THE LITTLE

BLACK BOOK OF

BEER

• *The Essential Guide to the Beloved Brewski* •

RUTH CULLEN

ILLUSTRATED BY KERREN BARBAS

PETER PAUPER PRESS, INC.
WHITE PLAINS, NEW YORK

For the love of beer

Special thanks to Mike Bayette and the
New England Beverage Company for the beer and the wisdom.
Thanks also to Linda Peer Groves, Dave Wecker, Dan Swinchuck,
Dick "Bumpy" Williams, and Frank Mandriotta,
for the devoted field work.

Responsible drinking is everyone's personal responsibility.

Designed by Heather Zschock

Illustrations copyright © 2005 Kerren Barbas

Visit us at www.peterpauper.com

THE LITTLE
BLACK BOOK OF

BEER

CONTENTS

INTRODUCTION

Beer is perhaps the most indispensable substance ever known to man.

So much more than a fermented malt beverage, beer has served as food and drink, medicine and currency. It conditions our hair and even kills slugs in our gardens.

We drink it at weddings and funerals, parties and ball games, and always feel just a little smarter, wittier, and more attractive when beer's around. When we wear beer goggles, everyone else seems that way, too.

A truly divine spirit, still brewed by monks and other holy folks, beer may indeed be proof that God loves us.

Today, for the first time in nearly a century, Americans have real choices to make when selecting their beer. The craft brewing renaissance has flooded the market with quality traditional beers and unique specialty brews, and even the most fervent of beer lovers can get overwhelmed.

Relax—you've got the cliff notes. With *The Little Black Book of Beer* in your back pocket, you have a world of beer knowledge at your fingertips. Never again will you freeze in panic before the beer cooler; you'll simply grab your handy reference guide and make an informed choice.

And that's what life's about, isn't it? Smart choices. Good beer. Cheers!

R. C.

ancient, heavenly beer:

BEER HISTORY AT A GLANCE

I feel wonderful drinking beer; in a blissful mood, with joy in my heart and a happy liver.

Sumerian Poem, 3000 B.C.E.

THE BIRTH OF BEER

The discovery of beer went something like this:

ANCIENT SUMERIAN WOMAN #1:
"Oh, my gourd! Here are those grains I left sitting out in the rain two weeks ago!"

ANCIENT SUMERIAN WOMAN #2:
(gasp) "What's that brown, frothy stuff where the rainwater should be?"

ANCIENT SUMERIAN WOMAN #1:
"The Goddess only knows. *(pause)* I dare you to taste it."

ANCIENT SUMERIAN WOMAN #2:
"Well, like my mother used to say, what doesn't kill you makes you stronger. Cheers!"

And so, life began—life *with* beer, that is.

Cultural anthropologists speculate that some ancient nomad stumbled upon a liquid of fermented grains and, intrigued, took a sip. The bitter-tasting brew was strangely pleasing, and each successive sip induced a sense of warmth, well-being, and extreme happiness—even giddiness.

There was only one explanation for this magical amber liquid: a gift from the earth mother. And, clearly, there was only one thing for our ancestors to do: make more of it.

CIVILIZING THE MASSES

Beer has a way of bringing people together.

Indeed, beer may have inspired the very first civilization by turning ancient humans away from hunter-gathering in order to pursue agriculture. By cultivating barley and other cereal grains for the purpose of making beer, the people of ancient Sumeria were assured a steady supply of "liquid bread."

A nutritious food and refreshing beverage, beer played an important role in the diet of these early humans. Unbeknownst to them, the process of fermentation—by which yeast transforms sugars into alcohol and carbon dioxide— quadrupled the vitamins and minerals in barley, and the wild yeasts supplied even more vitamins and proteins.

In all likelihood, our ancestors knew that beer kept them healthy and made them feel happy. And that was perfectly fine with them.

WOMEN'S WORK

RELIGIOUS MYTHS FROM ANCIENT CULTURES MAINTAIN THAT BEER was a gift from goddesses to women. For centuries, women were divinely inspired to brew beer and guard its secrets.

The earliest female brewers, or brewsters, were priestesses who created potent brews by first chewing barley before adding it to water, herbs, and spices in the brew pot. This chewed mash contained the enzyme ptyalin from their saliva, which helped convert grain starches into fermentable sugars, thus enhancing the strength of the beer. Brewsters also made beer by soaking half-baked loaves of barley bread in water, then straining the liquid, and aging it in clay containers sealed with mud.

The mysterious transformation from barley water to beer was attributed to the goddesses, and all cultures praised different deities for the beer they brewed and enjoyed—the goddess Ninkasi for the Sumerians, the goddess Ceres for the Romans, the goddess Isis (and her husband, Osiris), for the Egyptians.

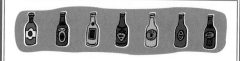

Drink like an Egyptian

The ancient Egyptians were the first to commercially brew beer, using it in religious and social ceremonies and even as a form of currency with which to pay taxes to pharaohs and wages to pyramid laborers. Ancient Egyptian writings hail beer for its medicinal qualities and illustrate how deeply ingrained it was in all aspects of their culture.

In addition to brewing at home, women sold their beer in taverns, or what we now know as brewpubs. The "alewives" of medieval Europe briefly enjoyed success and financial independence before they became a target of jealous rulers, who enacted laws imposing hefty taxes on both the production and sale of beer.

It was not long before the church got in on the action, establishing the first commercial breweries of Europe in monasteries that not only supplied the monks with daily rations of beer but also attracted legions of worshipers.

Ale-elujah!
God Bless Beer

BREWING AND DRINKING BEER continued to bring people closer together—and to God—throughout the Middle Ages, as monks supplied "church ale" to the masses and sold it to travelers.

Independent brewers, as opposed to the commercial enterprises controlled by the church, had to pay high taxes to brewing guilds, conveniently run by bishops, or face harsh punishments. If evading taxes didn't get brewers punished, the crime of making a bad beer certainly would:

Whoever makes a poor beer is transferred to the dung-hill.

Edict, City of Danzig, 11th century

Everyone drank beer. It was not only nutritious but also far safer than water since fermentation destroyed all of water's potentially harmful contaminants. For this reason, women continued to homebrew beers of various alcoholic strengths for all family members, including children—from low alcohol "small beers" to stronger ales.

While different cultures experimented with regional herbs, spices, and sweeteners to flavor their brews, the Germans went to great lengths to keep their beer pure. In 1516, Duke Wilhelm IV instituted a "beer purity law" known as the Reinheitsgebot, which restricted the ingredients in beer to malted barley, hops, and water (malted wheat and yeast were permitted at a later date).

Did You Know?

By the 18th century many colleges had their own brewhouses to supply beer to the students. Room and board could be paid with malted barley.

beer in the red, white, and blue

Those who drink beer
will think beer.

Washington Irving

REVOLUTION EVOLUTION:
IN BEER WE TRUST

It might well be true that the seeds of democracy were sown in beer.

Beer kept the Pilgrims afloat, although its short supply onboard the *Mayflower* possibly forced them to settle in Plymouth, Massachusetts—not their original destination of Virginia. Upon the Pilgrims' arrival, however, they quickly constructed brew houses to fortify their settlements with good old English ale. And when barley crops proved ill-suited to the cold, rocky soil of New England, they improvised and developed New World brews using maize (corn), pumpkin, and sassafras.

Commercial and home-brewing flourished in America from Colonial times all the way to the dark days of Prohibition, gaining momentum after the Revolutionary War with the blessing of our country's founders—

James Madison, Samuel Adams, and John Hancock.

George Washington and Thomas Jefferson were home brewers who espoused the benefits of beer, and even the melody of "The Star-Spangled Banner" sounds strikingly similar to a song sung in English alehouses.

The influx of German immigrants in the 19th century brought new styles of brewing to America, most notably the lighter, clean-tasting lager style of beer. Germans soon dominated the American brewing industry, establishing major brewing centers in Milwaukee, Philadelphia, Brooklyn, and St. Louis.

WHY ASK WHY:
PROHIBITION, DEPRESSION, AND SEDUCTION

Absence makes the thirsty grow thirstier.

The prohibition of alcohol made official by the Volstead Act in 1920 sent even the major brewers scrambling to stay in business. For 13 long dry years, the few breweries that survived did so by manufacturing non-alcoholic "near beers" and various other products like malt extracts, syrups, candy, and ice cream.

The end of Prohibition in 1933 marked a new beginning for beer, though not a particularly good one. The country was in the midst of the Great Depression, and to make beers that were both profitable and affordable, brewers had no choice but to add cheaper cereal grains like rice and corn to their malts.

The resulting beers were bland and tasteless compared to traditional European styles, but despite their compromised state, the brewing giants—especially Anheuser-Busch and Miller—have since then been enjoying tremendous success thanks to clever advertising in a nation thirsty for beer.

Lured by seductive ads with macho images and catchy phrases like, "For all you do, this Bud's for you" and "It's Miller time," Americans sidled up to the bar and, for years, never thought too much about what they were drinking.

MICRO STEPS IN THE RIGHT DIRECTION

In the 1960s, all you needed was love—of beer.

And a fellow named Fritz Maytag—of the washing machine and refrigerator Maytags—nurtured his love of good, quality beer by buying the struggling Anchor Steam Brewery and reacquainting Californians with old world-style ales.

In the early '70s, the lack of European-style ales in the U.S. drove a fellow Californian named Jack McAuliffe to brew his own. He fashioned a mini-brewing system, hired a professional beer scientist, and produced New Albion Ale and several other brews.

Though New Albion ultimately failed, the microbrewery concept took off, inspiring countless others to brew hand-crafted, unique beers with quality ingredients and revolutioning the way Americans approached their beer.

21ST CENTURY BREWS:
BEER, BEER EVERYWHERE BUT WHICH DROPS SHOULD YOU DRINK?

Today, beer remains a gift from the gods—divinely inspired, reverently worshiped.

Americans experienced a beer epiphany, of sorts, when they tuned in to what they were drinking and saw the light about real beer—that is, flavorful, old-style brews made with quality ingredients by traditional methods.

And although the mass-producing beer conglomerates still enjoy a huge market share in the beer industry, store shelves now boast astounding numbers of new, uniquely American craft beers and a wide selection of imports from around the world.

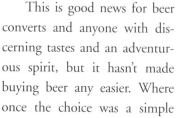

This is good news for beer converts and anyone with discerning tastes and an adventurous spirit, but it hasn't made buying beer any easier. Where once the choice was a simple toss-up between "light" or "regular" bubbly tan stuff in cans, nowadays there's a rainbow of bottled coppers, chocolate browns, and golden ambers adorning store shelves, not to mention a world of specialty brews available on tap at microbreweries and brew pubs across the nation.

So how does one begin to negotiate the wall of beer down at your local bar or beverage store? The first step involves taking a closer look at what's in your glass.

Who's Brewing Your Beer?

BREWPUB: Both a small brewery and a pub, brewpubs produce small quantities of hand-crafted beers and sell them on-site in a pub or restaurant, and sometimes in refillable, take-home gallons or half-gallon jugs.

MICROBREWERY: Relatively small breweries producing under 50,000 barrels of beer per year, microbreweries sell specially-crafted beers to various retail outlets and occasionally operate their own brewpubs. Some (technically former) microbreweries now produce larger volumes of beer and are considered craft brewers, due

to their careful brewing methods and use of quality ingredients.

CONTRACT BREWERY: Individual brewers, when constrained by space or production capabilities, contract with other production facilities, or contract breweries, to make beer for them. Many so-called "imports" or domestic brews that boast water from clear mountain springs are actually made far from their place of origin. Guinness Extra Stout, for example, is imported from Toronto, and Samuel Adams beer is made by the Boston Beer Company in Cincinnati and other locations, as well as in Boston!

COMMERCIAL BREWERY: With huge production capabilities, commercial breweries produce beer on a large scale for distribution and export. America's biggest breweries, Anheuser-Busch and Miller, annually produce well over 50 million barrels of beer apiece. Despite markedly lower production, foreign breweries with export capabilities often fall into this category.

know thy beer, know thyself

When the beer is in the man
Is the wisdom in the can?

Old Dutch saying

Upon reaching the legal drinking age, many young adults choose to further their education with a kind of independent beer study not offered during their years of schooling. But while these conscientious students pursue their thirst for beer knowledge with wild abandon, they—like countless adults—know virtually nothing about the beer they drink.

Learning some basic differences between beer styles may inspire you to re-start your independent beer study and quench your thirst with new and interesting beers from around the world.

ALES, LAGERS, AND IN-BETWEENS

 MOST BEERS FALL INTO TWO MAIN CATEGORIES: ales and lagers. Although the terms are used interchangeably to mean "beer," ales and lagers are fundamentally different due to the species of yeast used to make them.

All traditional beers were ales fermented by wild yeasts naturally existing in the environment, similar to the types of yeast found in wine and yogurt. These top-fermenting yeasts rise to the surface of liquids during fermentation, which occurs at warmer temperatures in just a matter of days.

Ales are generally fruity, complex, and heavier-tasting beers best served cool (50-60° F). Today, some of the most flavorful beers are made with top-fermenting ale yeasts, but only the Belgian lambic style beers are made the old-fashioned way with naturally occurring wild yeasts.

Lager beers, from a German word meaning "to store," are made with bottom-fermenting yeasts that ferment at the bottom of liquids at colder temperatures over a period of four or more weeks. Lagers are typically clear, crisp, and cleaner tasting than ales, and are meant to be drunk cold (at 40-50° F).

The pilsner style lager, famous for its extremely light and clean taste, was first brewed in Pilsen, Bohemia (now the Czech Republic) in 1842. The original Pilsner Urquell brand, though widely imitated, remains the benchmark of this classic style.

Other specialty beers may be distinguished by the manner in which they are brewed or the addition of special flavorings. Steam beers, for example, are made with lager yeasts brewed at ale temperatures. Smoked beers derive their unique flavor and aroma from malt that has been dried over wood smoke. And the addition of fruit during the fermentation process imparts a wine-like flavor to many fruit beers.

BEER STYLES

BEER STYLE / ALCOHOL BY VOLUME	CHARACTERISTICS

ALES

Barley Wine 8.4 - 12.0%	Strong, dark, and full-bodied with bittersweet, wine-like characteristics
Bitter Ale 3.0 - 5.8%	Light-bodied and distinctively bitter; ranging in strength and hop intensity from Ordinary to Best to Extra Special (ESB)
Brown Ale 4.0 - 6.4%	Sweet, malty, and medium-bodied with light hop presence
Mild Ale 3.2 - 4.0%	Mildly sweet, light-bodied, and low in hops and alcohol
Pale Ale 4.0 - 6.0%	Dry, hoppy, and medium-bodied with good malt balance
India Pale Ale (IPA) 5.0 - 10.5%	Strong, dry, and medium-bodied with intense hop aroma and bitterness

BEER STYLE / ALCOHOL BY VOLUME	CHARACTERISTICS

ALES

Strong Golden Ale 7.0 - 11.0%	Light-bodied and highly alcoholic with subtle flavors of fruit, spices, and hops
Old Brown and Red Ale 4.6 - 5.2%	Intensely sour, sweet, and wine-like with complex fruit and malt flavors
Old/Strong Ale 6.0 - 11.0%	Strong, dark, and full-bodied with rich fruit and malt flavors
Scottish Ales 2.8 - 8.0%	Dark, malty, and sweet, ranging in body and strength from light to "wee heavy"
Irish Red Ale 4.0 - 6.0%	Sweet, medium-bodied, reddish amber ale with caramel malt flavors and medium hop bitterness
Porter 4.5 - 6.0%	Dark, bitter, and light-bodied with roasted coffee and chocolate flavors
Stout 3.0 - 12.0%	Very dark, bitter, and medium-bodied with roasted coffee and chocolate flavors

BEER STYLE / ALCOHOL BY VOLUME	CHARACTERISTICS

ALES

Trappist/Abbey Ales 5.0 - 10.0%	Fruity, spicy, and strong with complex flavors and earthy, hoppy aromas
Saison & Bière de Garde 4.5 - 9.0%	Fruity, spicy, and dry with earthy, floral aromas
Wheat Beer 2.5 - 5.5%	Crisp and light-bodied with fruit and spice flavors
Lambic 5.0 - 7.0%	Intensely dry and fruity with complex earthy, cider-like flavors

LAGERS

Bock Beers 6.0 - 14.4%	Strong, full-bodied, and malty with mild sweetness and hopping
Dortmunder/ Export Lager 5.0 - 6.0%	Crisp, golden, and medium-bodied with good malt presence and light hopping
Dark and Black Lagers 3.8 - 5.0%	Dark and well-balanced with roasted malt flavors, hop bitterness, and a clean, dry finish

BEER STYLE / ALCOHOL BY VOLUME	CHARACTERISTICS

L A G E R S

Pilsner 4.0 - 6.0%	Dry, hoppy, and light-bodied with good hop aromas and flavors balanced by malt
Non-Alcoholic Lager <.5%	Mildly sweet, light-bodied, and highly carbonated with trace amounts of alcohol
Light, Low Carb, Dry, and Ice Lagers 4.0 - 6.0%	American variations of pilsner style. Mildly sweet, light-bodied, and highly carbonated with low malt and hop presence. Dry lagers have less sweetness, and ice lagers are higher in alcohol
Pale Lager (Helles) 4.5 - 5.5%	Medium-bodied and golden with toasted malt flavors and low bitterness
Amber/Red Lager 3.5 - 5.9%	Mildly sweet with toasted malt flavors and low hop presence
Malt Liquor 6.25 - 7.5%	High in alcohol with very low malt or hop flavors

SPECIALTIES & COMBINATION STYLES

Steam Beer 4.0 - 5.4%	Clean-tasting and medium-bodied with caramel malt flavors and moderate hop bitterness
Altbier 4.3 - 5%	Smooth and medium-bodied with crisp hop bitterness and good malt presence
Kölsch 4.8 - 5.3%	Pale, light-bodied, and mildly fruity with low hop bitterness
Smoked Beer 4.6 - 6.3%	Full-bodied and malty with smoky aromas and flavors
Fruit Beer 2.5 - 12%	Crisp and fruity with flavors ranging from very dry to sweet
Cream Ale 4.2 - 5.6%	Light-bodied, mild, and slightly sweet with low hop presence
Spiced/Flavored Beers 2.5 - 12%	Varying in intensity and strength, and flavored by assorted spices, vegetables, honey, and other substances

what's in a beer?

The mouth of a
perfectly contented man
is filled with beer.

—*Ancient Egyptian inscription*

FROM BREW TO BOTTLE:
THE ART OF MAKING BEER

Double, double toil and trouble;
Fire burn, and cauldron bubble.

Shakespeare, Macbeth

GREAT BEERS ARE BORN, NOT MADE, and the best brewers channel the talents of artists, chemists, chefs, maestros, and lovers to create masterpieces in malt.

Brewing requires the thoughtful selection and artful combination of ingredients, precise measurement, skillful technique, and timing, timing, timing.

The simple combination of four primary ingredients—malted barley, hops, yeast, and water—is anything but simple. But, like coffee, the heart and soul of a beer lies in its beans—well, grains, to be exact.

AMBER WAVES OF BARLEY

People have moxie, beer has malt.

 Malted barley gives beer flavor, color, and personality, as well as carbonation and alcohol when it has been mixed with yeast. The process of malting involves soaking barley grains in water until germination, then heating them to a desired level of dryness before grinding them into grist.

Several factors contribute to the characteristics of the malt, but especially the variety of barley used (expensive two-row barley or cheaper six-row) and the degree to which the barley is heated (e.g., dried, toasted, burnt). Other factors add levels of intricacy to the malting process that affect the beer's flavor, such as how the barley is heated (e.g., kiln, wood fire), and the proportions in which different malts are blended.

As the ancient Sumerians discovered so long ago and the Germans crafted into law, barley is best suited for brewing and serves as the foundation for most beers—although wheat makes a fine alternative. Other inexpensive cereal grains like corn and rice are widely used by big beer manufacturers, and, for centuries, people have experimented with just about everything else.

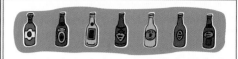

Common Malts Used in Brewing

BLACK MALT: deep, black color; sharp, burnt, espresso flavors

BROWN MALT: light brown color; warm, bready flavors

CARAMEL AND CRYSTAL MALTS: reddish hues; sweet caramel flavors

CHOCOLATE MALT: chocolate-brown color; coffee and caramel flavors

LAGER MALT: pale in color; clean and light tasting

PALE ALE MALT: straw colored; "biscuity" cracker-like flavors

VIENNA AND MUNICH MALTS: amber hues; sweet, nutty flavors

WHEAT MALT: light in color; fruity and spicy flavors

JUICING THE GRAIN

YOU CAN'T JUDGE A BARLEY BY ITS COVER, because inside every pebble-like grain is a sweet, sugary syrup dying to get out.

Brewers mix barley malt with water to make "mash," and heat it in a large vessel called the "mash tun" to extract fermentable sugars. Not all water is created equal, so brewers often adjust the mineral content and alkalinity (pH) of their water to ensure consistency in the brews they create.

After a period of time at various temperatures regulated by the brewer, the liquid "wort" (wërt) is strained from the solid matter, and poured into a large metal brew kettle, where the actual boiling and "brewing" takes place. The sugar content of the wort is known as "original gravity," and beers with high original gravity will have correspondingly higher alcohol content.

In the brew kettle, the wort is diluted and boiled, and the brewer often adds hops, the bitter, herbaceous flowers of the hop plant, *humulus lupulus*. A close relative of *cannabis sativa,* or marijuana, hops have mild sedative qualities but are primarily used for their floral and preservative qualities. Hop bitterness balances the sweetness of the malt, adding to the aroma, complexity, and sharpness of the beer, and hop tannins help stabilize and preserve the beer.

Hops may be used in pellet form, extracts, or dried whole flowers, and different varieties of hops are valued for their floral, bitter, earthy, or sometimes fruity characteristics. Cascade hops, for example, are grown in the Pacific Northwest and impart distinctively bitter, floral, citrus flavors and aromas.

Aside from hops, the brewer may add other herbs and spices to the brew kettle, such as juniper, coriander, or cloves, before filtering and transferring the wort to a large fermentation vessel for a period of aging known as fermentation.

A Word on "Cold Filtering"

All beers are filtered cold, if they're filtered at all. Low, near freezing temperatures help separate yeast solids from the beer, and "cold filtering" is standard industry protocol. American mega brewers typically over-filter their beers in the name of "smoothness."

THE FERMENTATION TRANSFORMATION

Until yeast is added to the liquid in the fermentation vessel, the beer is not yet an ale or a lager.

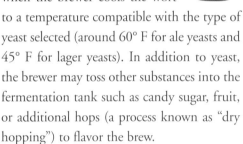

Primary fermentation begins when the brewer cools the wort to a temperature compatible with the type of yeast selected (around 60° F for ale yeasts and 45° F for lager yeasts). In addition to yeast, the brewer may toss other substances into the fermentation tank such as candy sugar, fruit, or additional hops (a process known as "dry hopping") to flavor the brew.

Top-fermenting ale yeasts produce a white, creamy head as they rise to the surface of the beer during the course of a week, and impart a wide range of complex, fruity flavors. Bottom-fermenting lager yeasts eat their way to the bottom of the liquid over a period of weeks or months, producing beer that is clearer and cleaner.

Regardless of the type of yeast employed, when these hungry microorganisms devour sugars in the wort during fermentation, they produce alcohol and carbon dioxide—and also heat, requiring the brewer to carefully monitor and regulate the temperature of the beer.

Primary fermentation ends when the brewer cools the beer after it has attained a desirable concentration of residual sugars. At this point, a secondary fermentation may be encouraged in the fermentation tank with the addition of more yeast or partially fermented wort, a process known as krausening that helps to develop and refine the beer's flavors.

The brewer then cools the beer to near-freezing temperatures and may filter it to remove yeast proteins before transferring it to bottles, kegs, casks, or cans. Either before or after bottling, the beer may also be pasteurized to halt any additional yeast activity.

Some ales undergo secondary fermentations or "conditioning" inside bottles or casks with added sugar and yeast. Cask-conditioned English ales tend to be lightly carbonated—flat in comparison to mass-produced American beers which sport large, fast-rising bubbles due to injections of carbon dioxide.

Many German weissbiers and Belgian ales fizz like champagne when opened, and overflow with tiny, frothy bubbles that drape like lace on the inside of the glass. The presence of yeast often gives these ales a slight haze, and yeast sediment is usual- ly visible inside the bottle. Because these ales are "alive" and un-pasteurized, they require careful handling and storage to avoid spoilage.

For the Love of Beer:
A WORD ON HOMEBREWING

Give a man a beer and
he'll waste an hour.
Teach a man to brew and
he will waste a lifetime!

The Home Brew Company

Many beer enthusiasts turn their love of
drinking beer into a lifelong hobby of
brewing it. And who could blame them?
Homebrewing is fun, creative, and relatively easy to do—not to mention cost-
effective. For an initial investment of
about $100 for supplies and ingredients,

homebrewers realize significant cost savings after just a few batches and, best of all, get to drink the fruits of their labors.

Novice and experienced homebrewers can benefit from the wisdom and counsel of Charlie Papazian, a foremost authority on homebrewing and author of *The New Complete Joy of Homebrewing* and other beer tomes. Starter beer kits and all kinds of excellent resources abound online, and most can be found by simply entering "homebrew" or "brew" into an internet search engine.

Here are a few comprehensive beer sites, many with homebrewing links, to get you started:

www.beertown.org
(American Homebrewers Association)

www.byo.com
(*Brew Your Own* magazine)

www.beeradvocate.com
(*Beer Advocate* magazine)

www.allaboutbeer.com
(*All About Beer* magazine)

www.beerhunter.com
(Website of Michael Jackson, Beer Expert)

tasting and evaluating:

IT'S ALL IN THE APPROACH

Without question, the
greatest invention in the
history of mankind is beer.

Dave Barry

No Whining at the Bar

Attitude is everything—especially when it comes to how you approach beer. And thankfully, in this regard, beer isn't wine.

Leave your pretensions with the sommelier, because beer needs no fancy introduction, no pedigree, no "terroir." Rarely does beer need to "breathe," and only occasionally does it require a glass (such as when it's on tap from a cask or keg).

Beer is versatile and dependable, and you can always count on it to liven up the party or wind things down at the end of the day. Whether you're eating a burger and fries or  *foie gras* of goose, beer steps up to the plate and takes a swing, delivering home-run flavors and thirst-quenching goodness every single time.

But make no mistake: beer may be straightforward and direct, but it's not simple.

Au contraire! In terms of depth, complexity, and overall satisfaction, beer rivals—and often surpasses—the juice of the grape. Pharaohs, paupers, and average Joes have known this all along, and many others are just now beginning to see the sophistication and exceptional range of flavors found in traditional and contemporary styles of beer.

A Matter of Taste

Taste buds don't lie. You either like something or you don't.

The instant some putrid substance hits your tongue and odors waft into scent receptors in your nose, the party's over. Thanks for coming. Don't forget your coat.

When we slow down and pay close attention to sensations of sight, sound, smell, taste, and touch, the experience of eating or drinking becomes far more interesting and enjoyable.

Unfortunately, we Americans tend to like things big and fast, and, understandably, who has time to pay attention when you're jockeying for space at the all-you-can-eat buffet and chugging pitchers of Crud Light?

Drinking beer need not be like a hot dog eating contest, and tasting beer—truly savoring it and appreciating its finer qualities—

requires just a few simple observations.

Appearance

A beer's color gives you clues about its style, and the best way to accurately view color is through a clear glass. Any glass will do, but a medium-weight, tall glass with a wide mouth works well for most styles of beer.

● Tilt the glass to one side and carefully pour the beer down the inside of the glass. Allow the last inch or so of beer to pour directly into the center of the glass so that it produces a head of foam.

● Different beer styles and levels of carbonation produce varying degrees of foam. Does the head appear thick and creamy or thin and loosely held together? Are the bubbles fast-rising and quick to dissipate? Or are they the size of a pinhead and long lasting?

● Look at the color of the beer. Is

it light and pale or dark as molasses? Do you see straw-colored golds, cherry reds, or nut browns?

⬤ The clarity of a beer may indicate the presence of ale yeasts. Is the beer crystal clear, or does it appear somewhat hazy or cloudy?

Aroma

The aromas or "bouquet" of a beer reveals much about its flavors.

⬤ Swirl the beer to release its aromatics, then lean into your glass and take a big sniff, being careful not to snort any liquid into your nostrils.

⬤ Do you detect the scent of flowers? Pine trees? Grapefruit? Apples?

⬤ Does the beer smell sweet, smoky, or bready?

⬤ Do you smell spices like cinnamon or nutmeg?

Taste

The range of flavors in a beer contributes to its overall taste or "palate," and the way flavors relate to one another is called "balance." Taste is further influenced by the impression of a beer's texture, or body. Beers can be light-bodied, medium-bodied, or full-bodied.

● Inhale gently through your nostrils as you take a sip of your beer, allowing the liquid to roll over all areas of your tongue.

● Do you taste nutty sweetness, sharp bitterness, or sour fruit?

● Does the flavor remind you of fresh baked bread, burnt toast, or black espresso?

● Does the weight of the beer feel light and crisp, or thick and heavy?

Finish

The lasting impression a beer leaves on your senses after you swallow is known as its "finish." The finish includes the lingering taste a beer leaves in your mouth, as well as the warming sensations it creates as you swallow it.

● Swallow a sip of beer, and note the way it feels as it travels down your esophagus.

● Does your mouth feel crisp and refreshed? Or is there a distinctly bitter, malty, or yeasty (bready) aftertaste?

Good Beer Flavors

- Bitter
- Burnt
- Caramel
- Earthy
- Fruity
- Malty
- Bready
- Coffee
- Floral
- Nutty

Bad Beer Flavors

- Chemical
- Moldy
- Plastic
- Skunky
- Sulfury
- Metallic
- Musty
- Rusty
- Soapy
- Wet cardboard

Why Is Bitter Good?

Judging by the shape many Americans are in, the national sweet tooth needs to be yanked. We simply can't get our fill of sweets. And when we eat and drink predominantly sweet foods and drinks, we blunt our tastes for other, incredibly satisfying flavors: refreshingly crisp sours, mouthwatering salts. Taste buds detect bitterness, perhaps to serve as a warning before we swallow some noxious substance. In varying degrees, bitter isn't bad—it's good, better, and *best*. Think milk chocolate, dark chocolate, and special dark chocolate. Or, consider regular coffee, Starbucks coffee, and espresso. In beer, bitterness may come from roasted malts or hops, and in proper balance, it can provide the backbone, body, and bite essential to rounding out a beer's flavors.

GOOD DRINKING SENSE

SOME BEERS TASTE SO SMOOTH AND REFRESHING THAT YOU CAN'T HELP but toss back your head, drain your glass, and quickly pour another. But beer is not lemonade, a simple truth often learned the hard way after we quaff too many seemingly benign brews, only to discover later how truly potent they were. Light-colored beers are not necessarily light-tasting, nor are they low in alcohol. Some of the most alcoholic beers are pale, such as Belgian golden ale and malt liquor. Dark beers are not all heavy and strong, although some barley wines, English-style old ales, and bock beers pack about as strong a punch as beer can deliver. The best way to meet all your beery expectations is to know what you're drinking— and that means learning the characteristics of the

beer style, and being especially mindful of alcohol content.

People drink beer for different reasons—to quench thirst, complement food, celebrate with friends, or get drunk.

The alcohol in beer will indeed make you drunk if you drink enough of it, so, like any other alcoholic beverage, beer should be consumed in moderation, and should certainly be avoided before operating heavy equipment such as wrecking balls, monster trucks, or nose hair trimmers. Read any label on any beer bottle or can for general precautions about alcohol, as required by law.

To summarize: You really don't need a

reason to reach for a cold one, but if you want to fully appreciate the beer in your glass, you should pay attention to four main things—appearance, aroma, taste, and finish.

RESPECTFUL SERVICE:
TIPS ON BEER STORAGE, SERVING TEMPERATURE, AND GLASSWARE

BEER IS A PRODUCT WITH a shelf life, and the way you store it and serve it can make a big difference in how it tastes. Most beer labels indicate "serve-by" dates as well as optimum serving temperatures.

Light and heat can interact with the hops in beer, giving it a skunky, spoiled taste, and beers in clear or green glass bottles are especially susceptible to ultra-violet light damage. To keep your beer fresh, always store it upright in a cool, dark place like a cellar or refrigerator.

As a general rule, when serving several styles of beer during the course of an evening, light-colored beers come first, then darker and more flavorful brews. Top-fermented ales and robust lagers are served warmer so their fruity or full malt flavors

can be best appreciated. Serve American-style lagers, pilsners, and wheat beers at cooler temperatures (40-50° F), and heavier English-style ales, Trappist and abbey ales, and doppelbocks cool to warm (50-60° F).

Ideally, the glasses in which you serve beer should be hand-washed, as dishwashers often leave a slight residue that minimizes the natural head of a beer. Beyond that, the glass should allow you to see the beer and admire its color and head.

Many breweries design specific glasses to suit individual beer styles: tall, hourglass-shapes to encompass the voluminous head of many wheat beers; slender flutes for crystal-clear, golden pilsners; stemmed, tulip-shaped glasses for Belgian golden ales and other specialties. In their absence, white wine glasses or champagne flutes may be used for lighter colored beers, and red wine glasses, brandy snifters, or goblets for darker colored beers. Of course, the "right" glass is any glass, cup, or mug that makes for a pleasant drinking experience.

your guide
to beer styles

Give me a woman
who loves beer and I will
conquer the world.

Kaiser Wilhelm

THE FOLLOWING SECTION INCLUDES A SHORT, general description of each beer style, as well as tasting recommendations and food pairings.

There are simply too many excellent beers to list here by name, but in general, your local microbrews are the freshest and the best. With a few exceptions, the beers identified in this book are widely available and representative of each beer style.

Did You Know?

For hundreds of years, wedding celebrations were incomplete without "bride's ale," (the origin of the word "bridal"), which was sold on wedding days to enliven the festivities and increase the bride's dowry.

ales

I would give all my fame
for a pot of ale . . .

Shakespeare, Henry V

THE BEERS IN THE ALE FAMILY MAKE UP SOME OF THE MOST INTERESTING AND COMPLEX BEERS in the world. Top fermenting yeasts generally impart more expressive, fruity flavors that create layers of flavor when balanced by different malts and hop varieties.

Traditional European-style ales are now being brewed in growing numbers by North American craft brewers, with special emphasis on the distinctive hop varieties of the Pacific Northwest. True Belgian-style ales can be considered a category unto themselves, with unique flavor profiles derived from their specific strains of yeast and the manner in which they are brewed.

Ales may be cloudy or clear, in colors ranging from gold to red to brown, and are generally drunk cool to warm in order to appreciate their range of flavors.

BARLEY WINE

REGION OF ORIGIN:
England

ALCOHOL BY VOLUME:
8.4-12.0%

CHARACTERISTICS: More like a fine port or sherry, barley wine is a strong, rich, lightly carbonated ale with a raisiny malt sweetness and powerful alcohol presence. Dense, fruity, and bittersweet, barley wines range in color from copper to mahogany, and are best served as an aperitif or nightcap. These potent, warming brews have a thick mouth feel and are designed for sipping and savoring. The best English barley wines can be aged for decades, but most American barley wine-style ales should be drunk within five years.

TASTING RECOMMENDATIONS:
Anchor Old Foghorn
Dogfish Head Olde School

Rogue Old Crustacean
Sierra Nevada Bigfoot
Victory Old Horizontal

FOOD PAIRINGS: gamy meats; strong cheeses; rich desserts

BITTERS

REGION OF ORIGIN: England

COMMON VARIATIONS: ordinary bitter; best bitter; extra special bitter (ESB)

ALCOHOL BY VOLUME: ordinary (3.0-3.7%); best (4.1-4.8%); ESB (4.8-5.8%)

CHARACTERISTICS: Available on tap in pubs throughout England, true bitters are cask-conditioned, mildly carbonated ales that are distinctly bitter (hence the name) with a sub-tle backdrop of grainy malt and fruit. Bitters are generally dry (not sweet), light-bodied, and low in alcohol, ranging in strength and hop intensity from ordinary to best to extra special. Straw-gold to reddish copper in color, bitters may now be purchased in cans or bottles, oftentimes with "widgets" that inject nitrogen into the beer to produce a thick, creamy head and greater carbonation.

TASTING RECOMMENDATIONS:
Fuller's ESB
Gritty's Best Bitter
Redhook ESB
Rogue Younger's Special Bitter
Pyramid Alehouse ESB

FOOD PAIRINGS: fish and chips; sharp cheeses; rich meats

BROWN ALE

REGION OF ORIGIN: England

COMMON VARIATIONS:
North American-style

ALCOHOL BY VOLUME:
English (4.0-5.5%); North American-style
(4.0-6.4%)

CHARACTERISTICS: Classic, English-style brown ale hails from northern England and is traditionally a mild, refreshing, light brown ale with nutty, sweet caramel flavors and light to moderate hopping. Medium-bodied and pleasantly malty, Newcastle Brown Ale defines this style and remains a bestselling brand in England and abroad. Darker, sweeter brown ales can be found throughout England, and many North American-style variations are now available, identifiable by their balance of roasted malt, chocolate, or nutty flavors with floral, citric American hops.

TASTING RECOMMENDATIONS:
Brooklyn Brown Ale
Newcastle Brown Ale
Pete's Wicked Ale
Samuel Smith's Nut Brown Ale

FOOD PAIRINGS: grilled, roasted, or stewed
meats; poultry

MILD ALE

REGION OF ORIGIN: England

COMMON VARIATIONS:
pale mild; dark mild

ALCOHOL BY VOLUME:
pale or dark (3.2-4.0%)

CHARACTERISTICS: Mild ales, named for their mildness in hop character (bitterness), are refreshing, slightly sweet, low alcohol brews with a clean, gentle taste. Ranging in color from light amber to dark brown, mild ales were once quaffed in large quantities by hardworking farm laborers. Quaffing them nowadays can be a challenge as they can be hard to find, but tradition-minded craft brewers may yet revive this once popular style.

TASTING RECOMMENDATIONS:
Banks's Mild
Gale's Festival Mild
Highgate Mild

Robinson's Dark Best Mild
Sainsbury Mild

FOOD PAIRINGS: lunch fare

PALE ALE

REGION OF ORIGIN:
England

COMMON VARIATIONS: North American-style; Belgian-style

ALCOHOL BY VOLUME: English (4.5-5.5%); North American (4.5-5.5%); Belgian (4.0-6.0%)

CHARACTERISTICS: True English-style pale ales can be considered a bottled form of cask-conditioned English bitter—only stronger and fruitier. Golden to copper in color, pale ales have a complex palate with earthy, fruity English hop aromas and flavors, a light, cracker-like maltiness, and a dry hop finish. Pale ales are medium-bodied, fully carbonated, and moderately strong.

American-style pale ales differ from the English original in their bold use of Cascade hops, home-grown in the Pacific Northwest. Biscuity malt flavors combine with brightly floral, citrus, and piney hop aromatics and flavors to create a crisp, pleasantly bitter, flavorful brew. Like many Americans, Cascade hops are bold and flashy; traditional European brewers tend to prefer more subdued varieties like Fuggles or Goldings.

Belgian-style pale ales can be loosely compared to English-style pale ales, but like most Belgian beer styles, they are unique due to the strains of yeast used to make them. Golden to dark amber in color, Belgian ales are generally fruity, spicy, and smooth-tasting brews with a subtle malt character and moderate hopping.

TASTING RECOMMENDATIONS:

Samuel Smith's Old Brewery Pale Ale

Tetley's English Ale

Morland's Old Speckled Hen

Anchor Liberty Ale

Cisco Whale's Tale Pale Ale

Hobgoblin Imported English Ale

Hooker American Pale Ale

Saranac Pale Ale

Sierra Nevada Pale Ale

De Rank XXX Bitter

FOOD PAIRINGS: red meats; roasted poultry; spicy foods

INDIA PALE ALE (IPA)

REGION OF ORIGIN: England

COMMON VARIATIONS:
North American-style;
imperial/double IPA

ALCOHOL BY VOLUME: English (5.0-7.5%); North American (5.5-6.3%);
imperial (7.9-10.5%)

CHARACTERISTICS: India Pale Ale is a stronger, hoppier version of pale ale, originally brewed for British troops in India. British brewers intentionally made a high gravity, potent brew preserved and bittered with huge amounts of hops to withstand the long, hot voyage overseas in the days before refrigeration. Pale gold to copper in color, English-style IPA is characterized by intense hop bitterness, flowery hop aromas and flavors, and medium maltiness. These days, North American craft brewers have revived the style with flair and personality, creating gold to amber-colored, medium-bodied beers that are high in alcohol and distinctively bitter. The best of the new American IPAs are assertively bitter, perfumed with fruity, flowery hops, and balanced with toasty malt.

TASTING RECOMMENDATIONS:
Dogfish Head 90 Minute IPA
Magic Hat Hi.P.A.
Rogue Imperial IPA
Stone Arrogant Bastard
Victory Hopdevil

FOOD PAIRINGS: rich meats; spicy foods; sharp cheeses

STRONG GOLDEN ALE

REGION OF ORIGIN: Belgium

ALCOHOL BY VOLUME: 7.0-11.0%

CHARACTERISTICS: Belgian Golden Ale ain't called Devil for nothing. Smooth, light-bodied, and honey-colored with a thick, creamy head of foam, Belgian golden ale is deceptively strong and surprisingly complex. This beer tastes remarkably light on the first sip, but soon reveals layers of spicy, fruity yeast flavors paired with hop bitterness and warmed with alcohol. The best-selling beer in Belgium, Duvel (DOO-vl), meaning devil, exemplifies the style and achieves its characteristic flavors and champagne-like fizz through an elaborate triple-fermentation process that continues until the bottle is opened.

TASTING RECOMMENDATIONS:

Duvel

Huyghe Delirium Tremens Belgian Ale

La Chouffe

Unibroue La Fin du Monde

FOOD PAIRINGS: seafood; salty or spicy foods

OLD BROWN AND RED ALE

REGION OF ORIGIN: Belgium

COMMON VARIATIONS: Flanders oud bruin; Flemish red

ALCOHOL BY VOLUME: oud bruin (4.8-5.2%); Flemish red (4.6-5.2%)

CHARACTERISTICS: Belgium is home to some of the world's most unique and interesting beers, due largely to its geographic location, sandwiched between wine-producing regions in France and brewers in Germany. Many Belgian beer styles seem to marry the characteristics of wine, champagne, and beer, resulting in highly unusual, distinctive flavors that are not for everyone. Both oud bruin (old brown) and red ales are extremely sour beers of moderate strength, often blends of young ales fermented in stainless steel tanks and old ales aged in unlined oak barrels that house dozens of yeast and bacterial strains.

Oud bruin ale of East Flanders is dark brown in color, very low in hop aromas or flavors, and sharply acidic, with hints of caramel and chocolate sweetness lurking on the palate.

West of Flanders, the red ales, also known as the Burgundies of Belgium, are deep, red-brown in color and arrestingly tart, with tannic, acidic oaky flavors mingling with earthy, sweet flavors. Many people find these beers to be incredibly light-bodied, refreshing, and thirst-quenching; others cut the acidity with sweeteners like grenadine syrup.

TASTING RECOMMENDATIONS:
Duchesse de Bourgogne
Liefmans Goudenband
Rodenbach Classic (Red)
Rodenbach Grand Cru
Val Dieu Brown

FOOD PAIRINGS: shellfish or grilled seafood; citric foods or sauces

OLD/STRONG ALE

REGION OF ORIGIN: England

ALCOHOL BY VOLUME:
6.0-11.0%

CHARACTERISTICS: Often viewed as a winter warmer, traditional English-style old ale is a dark, reddish-brown, full-bodied, malty sweet ale with rich flavors of currants, molasses, burnt toffee, and chocolate. Like a rare cognac or fine sherry, many old ales improve with age, and some are bottled with yeast and sugar so they can continue to evolve over time. A great sipping beer with an alcoholic punch, old ales make a fine accompaniment to dense foods and rich desserts.

TASTING RECOMMENDATIONS:
Theakston's Old Peculier
Thomas Hardy's Ale (Vintage dated)
Fuller's Vintage Ale
Gale's Prize Old Ale
J. W. Lees Harvest Ale

FOOD PAIRINGS: gamy meats; strong cheeses; chocolate

SCOTTISH ALES

REGION OF ORIGIN: Scotland

COMMON VARIATIONS: light; heavy; export; Scotch

ALCOHOL BY VOLUME: light (2.8-3.5%); heavy (3.5-4.0%); export (4.0-5.3%); Scotch (6.2-8.0%)

CHARACTERISTICS: Scottish ales are characterized by rich maltiness, with chewy-sweet toffee and butterscotch flavors and a dark brown color. Scottish ales range in body and strength, from the least expensive "sixty shilling" light-bodied ales to the strong, sometimes syrupy, higher alcohol "ninety shilling" ales. The very malty, full-bodied Scotch ales, also called "wee heavy" ales, once were a huge export from Edinburgh. These days, American craft brewers have tried their hand at the style, creating some interesting variations with peated malt and more hop presence.

TASTING RECOMMENDATIONS:
Belhaven Scottish Ale
Caledonian MacAndrew's Scotch Ale
Grant's Scottish Ale/Scotch Ale
McEwans Scotch Ale
Traquair House Ale

FOOD PAIRINGS: lamb and other roasted meats

IRISH RED ALE

REGION OF ORIGIN: Ireland

COMMON VARIATIONS: North American-style amber

ALCOHOL BY VOLUME: Irish (4.0-4.5%); American (4.5-6.0%)

CHARACTERISTICS: Ranging in color from light reddish amber to light brown, Irish red ales have moderately sweet, caramel flavors balanced by hop bitterness. North American microbrewers have popularized these medium-bodied beers, placing greater emphasis on hop aromas and flavors.

TASTING RECOMMENDATIONS:
Alaskan Amber
Anderson Valley Boont Amber Ale
Magic Hat Humble Patience
Murphy's Irish Amber
Pete's Wicked Red Rush

FOOD PAIRINGS: grilled, roasted, or stewed beef or pork

PORTER

REGION OF ORIGIN: England

ALCOHOL BY VOLUME: 4.5-6.0%

CHARACTERISTICS: Both porter and stout are dark, toasty beers with a bitter bite, but porter is the smoother, milder version of the two. Deep ruby to almost black in color, porters are light-bodied brews of moderate strength with big chocolate and coffee flavors matched with hop bitterness. Dry on the palate with a long, satisfying finish, porters were a bitter, bracing favorite in the British Isles and, like stout, were often combined with lighter colored pale ales to create the classic Black and Tan. Many excellent porters can be found these days, from classic English styles to new North American microbrews.

TASTING RECOMMENDATIONS:
Fuller's London Porter
Samuel Smith's Taddy Porter
Smuttynose Robust Porter

Yakima Grant's Perfect Porter
Pripps Carnegie Porter

FOOD PAIRINGS: oysters, scallops, and
other shellfish; barbecue; chocolate

STOUT

REGION OF ORIGIN: Ireland, England

COMMON VARIATIONS: sweet; dry; imperial (Russian)

ALCOHOL BY VOLUME: sweet (3.0-6.0%); dry (3.8-5.0%); imperial (7.0-12.0%)

CHARACTERISTICS: Stout is a deep, dark brown to black colored, medium-bodied brew with robust burnt chocolate and espresso flavors. Stout appears to pour dark and thick with a rich, creamy head of foam, but many varieties are surprisingly light in body and low in alcohol. Dry stout is best known as Guinness—the dry, light, heavily hopped Irish classic with delicious dark chocolate flavors and mild acidity. As stout was often prescribed to nursing mothers, the Irish referred to it as "mother's milk," and viewed it as a healthful tonic. Some brewers took the famous combination of stout and oysters a step further and mixed stout with oyster

extracts, creating a somewhat fishy-tasting, seaweedy beer known as oyster stout.

Sweet stouts are traditionally English, with "milk" and "cream" variations sweetened by actual milk sugars (lactose). Oatmeal stouts are typically smooth and silky, with just a touch of nutty, malt sweetness rounding out the roasted chocolate, coffee palate. Other stouts may be sweetened with maple and honey.

Imperial stouts are strong stouts originally brewed in England for export to the tsars of Russia. These black, fruity, burnt-tasting brews have rich malt flavors, high hop bitterness, and a warming finish.

TASTING RECOMMENDATIONS:
Anderson Valley Barney Flats Oatmeal Stout
Guinness Stout Draught (widget can)
Rogue Shakespeare Stout

North Coast Old Rasputin Russian
  Imperial Stout
Victory Storm King Stout

FOOD PAIRINGS: oysters, scallops, and
other shellfish; barbecue; chocolate

TRAPPIST/ABBEY ALES

REGION OF ORIGIN: Belgium

COMMON VARIATIONS: extra, dubbel, tripel

ALCOHOL BY VOLUME: extra (5.0%); dubbel (6.0-7.5%); tripel (7.0-10.0%)

CHARACTERISTICS: The term "Trappist" is an appellation, or designation of origin, that refers to a family of beers made by five Trappist monasteries in Belgium: Chimay, Westmalle, Orval, Westvleteren, and Rochefort. Trappist breweries make numerous different beers, but all tend to be strong, top-fermenting, bottle-conditioned ales with an aromatic bouquet and complex palate of fruit, spices, and earthiness. Brewed under the supervision of monks by age-old traditional

methods, these ales are a fascinating blend of flavors—cloves, plums, flowers, and rum. Sometimes wired and corked like champagne, Trappist ales produce volumes of tiny, creamy bubbles in a huge head and almost always have a yeasty haze. These golden-orange to dark brown colored ales, brewed in three different  strengths from the mild extra to the powerful tripel, are best served warm (about 55° F).

Several other Belgian abbeys license brewers to produce beers bearing their name. These abbey-style beers cannot be labeled "Trappist," although they closely resemble the style and offer a range of similarly delicious beers.

TASTING RECOMMENDATIONS:
Chimay Grande Reserve (Blue)
Corsendonk Abbey Brown
McChouffe Artisanal Belgian Brown Ale
Rochefort 10
St. Bernardus Tripel
Westmalle Tripel
Westvleteren 8

FOOD PAIRINGS: gamy or rich meats; fish; patés

SAISON AND BIÈRE DE GARDE

REGION OF ORIGIN: Belgium and France

ALCOHOL BY VOLUME: saison (4.5-9.0%); Bière de Garde (4.5-8.0%);

CHARACTERISTICS: Saison, or season, is the traditional farmhouse ale of Southern Belgium originally brewed in March to be consumed in late summer and fall. Usually flavored with star anise and dried orange peels, saison is an incredibly refreshing, tart, medium-bodied orangy brew with a rocky, white head that forms the classic "Belgian Lace" on the inside of the glass. Saison Dupont defines this style, but most saisons are spicy, fruity, and crisp golden-orange colored brews.

The Bières de Garde of northern France are "beers for keeping," and, like saisons, were brewed in the springtime to be consumed during the fall harvest. Bottled champagne-style with wires and corks, these top-fermenting ales may be gold to reddish brown, with spicy, floral aromatics, yeasty fruitiness, and more defined malt flavors.

TASTING RECOMMENDATIONS:
Duyck Jenlain
La Choulette Ambrée
Saison Dupont
St. Sylvestre 3 Monts

FOOD PAIRINGS: grilled or rich meats; citric/spicy foods; strong cheeses

WHEAT BEER

REGION OF ORIGIN: Germany and Belgium

COMMON VARIATIONS: weizenbier/weissbier; hefeweizen; kristalweizen; dunkelweizen; Berliner weiss; Belgian witbier; North American-style

ALCOHOL BY VOLUME: weizenbier (2.5-5.4%); hefe/kristal/dunkelweizen (4.9-5.5%); Berliner weiss (2.8-3.4%); witbier (4.8-5.2%); North American-style (3.5-5.5%)

CHARACTERISTICS: Brewed with approximately 40-60% malted wheat, wheat beers are generally light-bodied, low alcohol refreshers with high carbonation and a crisp, clean, tart taste. Sometimes referred to as "white" beers, many wheat beers, like "white" wines, are pale amber in color with citric, fruity flavors. Whether they are dark (dunkelweizen), light and filtered (krystalweizen), or cloudy with yeast and unfiltered (hefeweizen, meaning yeast and wheat), domestic and imported wheat beers are widely available and make especially satisfying summer drinks.

South German weizenbier (wheat beer), also known as weissbier (white beer), has distinctive clove, banana, and smoky aromas and flavors from the strain of yeast it employs. These fruity, spicy beers are light on the palate and are often served with a slice of lemon.

Berliner weisse, perhaps the lightest and most refreshingly tart wheat beer, gets its characteristic milky-white appearance and pleasantly sour, acidic flavors from a secondary "lactic" fermentation using the same strain of yeast used in yogurt. Many Berliners sweeten this low alcohol beer with a shot of raspberry syrup.

A strong lager brewed with wheat, weizenbock is viewed more as a winter wheat beer with smoky, rich malt flavors and aromas. (Read more about Bock-style beers on pages 111-113.)

Spiced with coriander and Curacao orange peel, Belgian witbier (white beer) appears almost white in color due to its short lactic fermentation and yeasty haze. Deliciously tart, fruity, and spicy, witbiers are brightly citric and slightly grainy due to a high unmalted (raw) wheat concentration.

TASTING RECOMMENDATIONS:
Aventinus
Hoegaarden Original White
Kindl Berliner Weisse
Ommegang Witte
Schneider Weisse Weizenhell
Weihenstephaner Hefe Weissbier

FOOD PAIRINGS: citric or spicy foods; brunch fare; salads

LAMBIC

REGION OF ORIGIN:
Belgium

COMMON VARIATIONS:
gueuze; fruit lambics

ALCOHOL BY VOLUME:
5.0-7.0%

CHARACTERISTICS: Lambic-style beers, from the historic brewing town of Lembeek, can best be described in one word: wild. Brewed in open fermentation vessels made of wood, lambics are the only remaining beer style spontaneously fermented by wild, airborne yeasts. Exceedingly sour and reminiscent of hard cider, lambics have sharp, funky, fruity flavors that linger on the palate. As they age, lambics lose some of their razor-like acidity but become increasingly complex. Brewed with about 30% un-malted wheat, straight lambics are low in carbonation, winy-tasting, and honey-amber in color.

Straight lambic is difficult to find these days, but gueuze (gërz), a blend of young and old lambics, can usually be found—sometimes in less traditional, filtered versions with added sweeteners. Lambics sweetened with candy sugar are called faro, while fruited lambics are brewed with fruit added to the fermentation vessel. The most common fruited lambics—kriek (made with cherries), and framboise (made with raspberries)—pour pink to deep red and are typically tart, dry, and distinctively winy.

Many American craft brewers offer wheat beers with fruit or fruit extracts added, but these beers differ significantly from lambics. (Read more about Fruit Beers on pages 131-132.) Like sharply pungent, veined cheeses, lambics are not for everyone. But they're definitely worth a try, if only for the experience of tasting a bit of living history.

TASTING RECOMMENDATIONS:
Boon Gueuze Mariage Parfait
Cantillon Rose de Gambrinus
Hanssens Artisanaal Oude Kriek
Lindemans Framboise
Dogfish Head Festiva Lente

FOOD PAIRINGS: seafood, pâtés, chocolate,
sweet cheeses

Who's Your Bud?

The real Budweiser beer hails from a brewery named Budejovicky Budvar in the Czech city whose German name is Budweis. Budweiser Budvar beer enjoyed a huge following in Europe in the mid 1800s and was known by its slogan, "The Beer of Kings." You can bet your Wiener schnitzel that the folks in Budweis were none too pleased to discover that a German immigrant named Adolphus Busch had started brewing a beer named "Budweiser" in his St. Louis brewery, and that he advertised it as "The King of Beers." Although the beers share little resemblance in flavor and character, legal wrangling continues to this day. Suffice it to say that you'd be hard pressed to find an American Budweiser in many parts of Europe.

lagers

Life, alas,
Is very drear.
Up with the glass!
Down with the beer!

Louis Untermeyer

WHEN THE AVERAGE AMERICAN THINKS OF BEER, he thinks of the pilsner-style lager—but definitely not the European-style originated by the Czechs long ago. For most of the last century, beer in America meant highly carbonated, mildly flavored, moderately alcoholic lagers with little differentiation between brands.

Thankfully, times are a'changing. North American craft brewers have re-introduced true pilsner-style and other lager beers, and more and more Americans have begun to notice these and many fine traditional imports. With their clean taste and subtle to strong malt and hop flavors, lager beers are undeniably worldwide favorites.

Lagers are generally clear (not cloudy), ranging in color from gold to red to dark brown, and designed to be drunk cold.

BOCK BEERS

REGION OF ORIGIN:
Germany

COMMON VARIATIONS:
bock; doppelbock; eisbock;
maibock; weizenbock

ALCOHOL BY VOLUME: bock (6.0-7.5%);
doppelbock (6.5-8.0%); eisbock (8.6-
14.4%); maibock (6.0-8.0%); weizenbock
(6.5-11%+)

CHARACTERISTICS: Bocks are strong,
malty, copper to dark brown colored lagers
with lots of toasted, bready flavors and mild
sweetness. Bocks ferment over a period of
eight weeks at very cold, near freezing temperatures, and then require a storage period
of at least six months. The term "bock" is
thought to have originated from the historic
town of Einbeck, but it also refers to a male
goat—appropriate since both goats and
bocks deliver quite a kick!

 Extra-strong double bocks, or doppelbocks, were popularized by Pauline monks who first created these full-bodied beers as "liquid bread" to be consumed during Lent. Paulaner brewery's Salvator doppelbock led the way for a slew of powerful, malty doppelbocks all named with the suffix "ator": Maximator, Triumphator, Animator. Today, the bock beer style includes some of the strongest beers in the world.

Maibocks are the drink of spring, with a sunny-bronze color and a stronger hop aroma and finish. Eisbocks, or ice bocks, are sweet, malty, and syrupy dessert-style beers brewed intentionally strong by freezing the beer and removing any ice; since alcohol freezes at lower temperatures than water, the resulting brews are concentrated and highly alcoholic. Eisbocks are not to be confused with North

American-style Ice Beers, a distant relative of the pilsner style.

TASTING RECOMMENDATIONS:

Aass Bock
Ayinger Celebrator Doppelbock
Einbecker Mai-Ur-Bock
Samuel Adams Triple Bock
Schneider Aventinus Weizen Eisbock

FOOD PAIRINGS: pasta; gamy meats; sweet or spicy foods

DORTMUNDER/EXPORT LAGER

REGION OF ORIGIN: Germany

ALCOHOL BY VOLUME: 5.0-6.0%

CHARACTERISTICS: Dortmund-style lager is a mildly hoppy, medium-bodied, deep golden colored beer with a firm malt flavor and clean, dry finish. Less aromatic and bitter than a pilsner, the slightly sweeter, maltier Dortmund-style lager was once exported throughout Europe.

TASTING RECOMMENDATIONS:
Dortmunder Actien Brauerei (DAB) Original
Gordon Biersch Export
Great Lakes Dortmunder Gold
Stoudt Export Gold

FOOD PAIRINGS: grilled meats and poultry; lunch fare

DARK (DUNKEL) AND BLACK (SCHWARZBIER) LAGERS

REGION OF ORIGIN: Germany

ALCOHOL BY VOLUME: dunkel (4.5-5.0%); schwarzbier (3.8-5.0%)

CHARACTERISTICS: Dunkels are dark brown, malty lagers with bread-like aromas and mildly sweet chocolate and roasted malt flavors. Clean and well-balanced, dunkels have just enough hop bitterness to counter the malt. Schwarzbiers are reminiscent of stouts in color and flavor, almost black in color with dark chocolate, coffee flavors and a tangy, dry finish. Like stouts, schwarzbiers are sometimes mixed with lighter beers to make lager versions of the Black and Tan.

TASTING RECOMMENDATIONS:
Ayinger Altbairisch Dunkel
Einbecker Schwarzbier

Kostritzer Schwarzbier
Sprecher Black Bavarian
Warsteiner Dunkel

FOOD PAIRINGS: pasta; sausages; grilled or stewed meats

PILSNER

REGION OF ORIGIN: Bohemia, Czech Republic

VARIATIONS: European-style; North American-style (light, low carbohydrate, ice, dry)

ALCOHOL BY VOLUME: European (4.0-5.0%); North American (4.3-6.0%)

CHARACTERISTICS: True Pilsner-style lager is a straw-gold brew perfumed with flowery hops and balanced by malt. Complex on the palate with a clean, dry finish, the original pilsner brewed in Pilsen, Bohemia, in 1842 was, due to its strain of bottom-fermenting yeast, noticeably lighter and clearer than beers of that time. When Pilsen brewers failed to trademark the style name, many copycat versions (pilsener/pils) soon became widely available and hugely popular.  Pilsner Urquell defines this style, though several other European-style pilsners and a handful of all-malt American craft brews show due reverence.

Unfortunately, most North American-style pilsners are bland, diluted versions of the original, best drunk ice-cold to make up in refreshment what they lack in flavor. Brewed with hops extracts and adjuncts like corn and rice to add sweetness and filler, American pilsners have virtually no bouquet and undetectable bitterness. These beers are highly filtered and artificially carbonated after an abbreviated period of aging. "Light," "low-carbohydrate," and "ice" styles are simply variations of this dismal American take on the original, albeit with fewer calories, lower carbs, or higher alcohol, respectively. "Dry" lagers, first brewed by Asahi in Japan and now by American mega brewers, are less sweet, highly carbonated, low alcohol pilsners without great depth or complexity.

TASTING RECOMMENDATIONS:
Asahi Dry Lager
Brooklyn Pilsner
Czechvar/Budvar
F. X. Matt Accel (low carb)
Pilsner Urquell

FOOD PAIRINGS: salty or spicy foods; seafood

NON-ALCOHOLIC LAGER

REGION OF ORIGIN: Europe

ALCOHOL BY VOLUME: <.5%

CHARACTERISTICS: Similar to the American-pilsner style, non-alcoholic lagers are typically sweet, highly carbonated, and lacking strong hop or malt character, though several flavorful examples have been developed in recent years. By law, non-alcoholic brews must contain less than half of one percent alcohol.

TASTING RECOMMENDATIONS:
Guinness Kaliber
Marke Clausthaler Lager
O'Doul's Amber

FOOD PAIRINGS: salty or spicy foods; grilled meats and poultry; pasta

PALE LAGER (HELLES)

REGION OF ORIGIN:
Germany

COMMON VARIATIONS:
Münchner-style helles

ALCOHOL BY VOLUME: 4.5-5.5%

CHARACTERISTICS: Munich-style helles is a straw to golden colored, medium-bodied beer that emphasizes toasty, bready malt flavors. Low in bitterness and not fragrantly hoppy like a pilsner, this beer is a popular everyday favorite of Bavarians, often consumed with breakfast.

TASTING RECOMMENDATIONS:
Augustiner Vollbier Hell
Pete's Helles Lager

FOOD PAIRINGS: brunch fare; mild seafood

AMBER/RED LAGER

REGION OF ORIGIN: Germany

COMMON VARIATIONS: Vienna-style lager; Märzen/Oktoberfestbier; North American-style amber

ALCOHOL BY VOLUME: German (4.8-5.9%); North American (3.5-5.4%)

CHARACTERISTICS: Reddish brown to copper in color, Vienna-style lagers are characterized by toasty malt aromas and flavors and mild malt sweetness. Märzen/Oktoberfest-style beers, brewed in March and stored until the October celebrations, are a shade lighter, more reddish-gold to bronze, and a touch sweeter. Toasty, juicy malt flavors are balanced with subtle hops, making these very smooth, drinkable brews.

Inspired by these German styles, North American amber lagers pour amber to copper in color and emphasize sweet, malt flavors. Where they differ is in the use of hops. Citric, brightly floral American hop varieties may be subtle or exaggerated in the nose and palate, depending on the brewer's preference. This slightly sweet, versatile lager satisfies the sweet tooth and pairs well with many popular American foods.

TASTING RECOMMENDATIONS:
Ayinger Oktoberfest-Märzen
Paulaner Oktoberfest Märzen
Spaten Oktoberfest Ur-Märzen
Thomas Hooker Oktoberfest

FOOD PAIRINGS: pizza; roasted, grilled, or stewed meats; sausages

MALT LIQUOR

REGION OF ORIGIN:
North America

ALCOHOL BY VOLUME:
6.25-7.5%

CHARACTERISTICS: Malt liquor is a high alcohol version of North American-style pilsner, with moderate sweetness, virtually no hop aroma or flavor, and barely perceptible bitterness. Not really a liquor and lacking any true malt flavors, whoever named this strong, unmalty beer "malt liquor" might first have sampled a few.

TASTING RECOMMENDATIONS:
Haffenreffer Private Stock
Imported Elephant Malt Liquor

FOOD PAIRINGS: salty or spicy foods; seafood or shellfish

specialties & combination styles

I will make it felony to
drink small beer.

Shakespeare, Henry IV

OTHER SPECIALTY BEERS MAY BE DIS-TINGUISHED by the manner in which they are brewed or by the addition of special flavorings. For example, steam beers are made with lager yeasts brewed at ale temperatures; smoked beers derive their unique flavor and aroma from malt that has been dried over wood smoke; and the addition of fruit during the fermentation process imparts a wine-like flavor to many fruit beers.

STEAM BEER (CALIFORNIA COMMON BEER)

REGION OF ORIGIN: United States

ALCOHOL BY VOLUME: 4.0-5.4%

CHARACTERISTICS: Steam beer, also known as California Common beer, gets its clean, round character and fluffy white head from a lager yeast that's brewed at warmer, ale temperatures. Amber in color and medium-bodied, steam beers have moderate hop bitterness balanced with caramel flavors and aromas. First brewed during the California Gold Rush, the trademark-named "steam beer" is made exclusively at Anchor Steam Brewing Company in San Francisco. It is the only style of beer indigenous to the United States.

TASTING RECOMMENDATIONS: Anchor Steam Beer

FOOD PAIRINGS: grilled meats; seafood; sourdough breads

ALTBIER AND KÖLSCH

REGION OF ORIGIN: Germany

ALCOHOL BY VOLUME: altbier (4.3-5.0%); kölsch (4.8-5.3%)

CHARACTERISTICS: The local favorite in the city of Dusseldorf, altbier, or old beer, is a medium-bodied, copper-brown brew with clean, rounded flavors and snappy hop bitterness. Brewed with various malts, including wheat, and fermented at cold, lager temperatures with an ale yeast, altbier's smooth malty body finishes crisp and dry.

Kölsch is a delicate, light-bodied, clean-tasting beer from the Cologne region of Germany. Warm fermented with an ale yeast, and aged at cold temperatures (sometimes with a lager yeast added to the bottle) kölsch may be brewed with up to 15% wheat malt, enhancing its fruity undertones and lightening its gold color to pale straw. Low in bitterness but with a drying, hop finish, kölsch is a refreshingly light and drinkable brew.

TASTING RECOMMENDATIONS:
Long Trail Double Bag (7.2% ABV)
Frankenheim Alt
Küppers Kölsch
Reissdorf Kölsch
Zum Uerige Altbier

FOOD PAIRINGS: roasted or grilled meats, sausages

SMOKED BEER (RAUCHBIER)

REGION OF ORIGIN: Germany

COMMON VARIATIONS: Scottish-style

ALCOHOL BY VOLUME: rauchbier (4.6-6.3%)

CHARACTERISTICS: Smoked beers derive their characteristic smoky aromas and flavors from malt that has been exposed to smoke from burning wood, usually beech wood, oak, or alder. These full-bodied, light to dark brown lagers taste mildly sweet, with low hop bitterness and a smooth but assertive smoky palate. Intense smokiness defines Scottish-style smoked beers, which use barley malt kilned over burning peat, the half-decayed plant matter removed from marshy areas and dried for fuel.

TASTING RECOMMENDATIONS: Alaskan Smoked Porter

Aecht Schlenkerla Rauchbier Märzen
Rogue Smoke Ale
Pyramid Tilted Kilt Ale

FOOD PAIRINGS: smoked or grilled foods;
sausages

FRUIT BEER

REGION OF ORIGIN: International

ALCOHOL BY VOLUME: 2.5-12.0%

CHARACTERISTICS: Fruit beers are American-style wheat beers fermented with fruit or fruit extracts that may be mild to intensely fruity in aroma and flavor, with palates ranging from very dry to quite sweet. The most interesting fruit beers are those brewed with whole fruit or fruit purees, not those featuring "natural fruit flavors." Although some fruit beers evoke the Belgian lambic style with their complex, sour palates, fruit beers use traditional wheat beer as a base and are not spontaneously fermented by wild yeasts.

TASTING RECOMMENDATIONS:
Bar Harbor Blueberry Ale
Long Trail Blackbeary Wheat
New Glarus Raspberry Tart
New Glarus Wisconsin Belgian Red

Samuel Adams Cherry
  Wheat Beer
Unibroue Éphémère

FOOD PAIRINGS: desserts,
chocolate; brunch fare

CREAM ALE

REGION OF ORIGIN:
United States

ALCOHOL BY VOLUME:
4.2-5.6%

CHARACTERISTICS: A relative of steam beer,
cream ale is a crisp, refreshing golden beer
with mild sweetness and low hop character.
Cream ales are sometimes blends of top and
bottom fermenting beers, or some combination of the two, fermented warm, and then
stored in cold temperatures.

TASTING RECOMMENDATIONS:
Genesee Cream Ale

Little Kings Cream Ale
Rogue Honey Cream Ale
Terrapin Extreme Cream
Wexford Irish Cream Ale

FOOD PAIRINGS: grilled seafood, meat, or poultry

SPICED, HERBED, AND OTHER SPECIALTY BEERS

REGION OF ORIGIN: International

COMMON VARIATIONS: herb, spice, vegetable, honey, chocolate, coffee

ALCOHOL BY VOLUME: 2.5-12.0%

CHARACTERISTICS: Flavoring beer with various herbs and spices is nothing new. In fact, some of the earliest beers were mead beers made with honey, giving them flowery, honey aromatics and subtle sweetness. Nowadays, craft brewers near and far continue to experiment with a wide range of flowers, vegetables,

roots, and seeds to impart distinctive flavors to their beer. The best flavored beers have balance between hop, malt, and whatever adjuncts are used: juniper berries, red chili peppers, pumpkin, coffee. Christmas beers usually sport the spicy aromas and flavors of cloves, nutmeg, coriander, ginger, spruce, and licorice. Beers brewed with a portion of malted rye tend to be dry and slightly grainy with a spicy, fruity palate and bitter rye finish.

TASTING RECOMMENDATIONS:
Buffalo Bill's Pumpkin Ale
Dogfish Head Midas Touch
Hitachino Nest 2004
Mexicali Rogue (chili beer)
Schierlinger Roggen Bier (Rye)

FOOD PAIRINGS: Match food with beer flavors (e.g., spicy foods with chili beer).

glossary of terms

Beauty lies in the hands
of the beer holder.

Anonymous

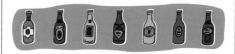

BALANCE: The degree to which a beer's flavors relate to one another. Desired balance of malt and hop flavors varies by beer style.

BODY: The weight of a beer in the mouth, described as light-bodied, medium-bodied, or full-bodied.

BOTTOM FERMENTED: Brewed with a type of yeast that sinks to the bottom of liquid during fermentation, which occurs at colder temperatures over a period of weeks or months. Bottom fermenting yeasts create smooth, clear, clean-tasting beers. Lagers are made with bottom fermenting yeasts.

CASK/BOTTLE CONDITIONED: Refers to beer that undergoes additional fermentation in bottles or casks with added yeast and, often, sugar. Cask/bottle conditioned beers are un-pasteurized, cloudy, and naturally carbonated.

FERMENTATION: The process by which yeast transforms sugars into alcohol and carbon dioxide.

FINISH: The resulting impression of a beer after it has been swallowed.

HOPS: Herbaceous flowers that give beer its bitter aromas and flavors. Hops have natural preservative and mild sedative qualities. Many different varieties of hops contribute different aromatic and flavor profiles in beer.

MALT: The most important ingredient in beer, usually made from barley that has been soaked until partial germination, dried or roasted to varying degrees, and ground into grist. Brewers combine different malts to create desired colors, flavors, and aromas.

PASTEURIZATION: The process by which a substance is heated to prevent further microbial activity.

REINHEITSGEBOT: The German "beer purity law" that restricts the ingredients in beer to malted barley or wheat, hops, yeast, and water. Many European and American craft brewers still follow this law and advertise their use of traditional ingredients on their beer labels.

TOP FERMENTED: Brewed with a type of yeast that rises to the top of liquid during fermentation, which occurs at warmer temperatures over a period of days. Top fermenting yeasts may impart fruity, spicy, and earthy aromas and flavors. Ales are made with top fermenting yeasts.

WORT: The unfermented liquid produced by "brewing," or boiling water, malt and hops, before yeast is added.

Life is
beer

INDEX